# HANDMADE THINKING

## A PICTURE BOOK
## ON
## READING AND DRAWING

### BY LAURENCE MUSGROVE

WWW.HANDMADETHINKING.COM
SAN ANGELO, TEXAS

ISBN-13: 978-1456450403
ISBN-10: 1456450409

TO
MARIE-CLARE

"WE CAN USE THE SIMPLICITY AND IMMEDIACY OF PICTURES TO DISCOVER AND CLARIFY OUR OWN IDEAS, AND USE THOSE SAME PICTURES TO CLARIFY OUR IDEAS FOR OTHER PEOPLE, HELPING THEM DISCOVER SOMETHING NEW FOR THEMSELVES ALONG THE WAY."

*THE BACK OF THE NAPKIN*, DAN ROAM

"DRAWING IS ONE OF THE SUREST MEANS OF ACQUIRING KNOWLEDGE."

*"DRAWING IN GENERAL EDUCATION,"* D. R. AUGSBURG

"IN FACT, WITHOUT VISUALIZATION, STUDENTS CANNOT COMPREHEND, AND READING CANNOT BE SAID TO BE READING."

*READING IS SEEING*, JEFFREY WILHELM

"WHAT IS MOST COMPELLING TO ME ABOUT THE ACT OF DRAWING IS THAT YOU BECOME AWARE, OR CONSCIOUS OF, WHAT YOU'RE LOOKING AT ONLY THROUGH THE MECHANISM OF TRYING TO DRAW IT."

*DRAWING IS THINKING*, MILTON GLASER

"TO ALL THE KIDS WHO QUIT DRAWING . . . COME BACK!"

*WHAT IT IS,* LYNDA BARRY

# *TABLE OF CONTENTS*

# BRIEF INTRODUCTION

I COMPOSED THIS **PICTURE BOOK** FOR TEACHERS TO EMPHASIZE THE **POWER OF DRAWING** AS A WAY TO IMPROVE STUDENTS' **READING** HABITS.

**MY PURPOSE** IS NOT TO SUGGEST AN **ALTERNATIVE**, BUT AN **ADDITIONAL** WAY FOR STUDENTS TO RESPOND TO TEXTS. WHEN WE TEACH STUDENTS TO USE **BOTH WORDS AND IMAGES** TO DISCOVER AND COMMUNICATE THEIR IDEAS, THEY ARE LEARNING **TWO DISTINCT** AND EQUALLY IMPORTANT **LANGUAGES**. THEY ARE, IN A WAY, BECOMING **BILINGUAL**.

I HAVE FOUND THAT STUDENTS READILY **EMBRACE** DRAWING WHEN RESPONDING TO WHAT I ASK THEM TO READ. AND **WHEN I SAY** "THAT STUDENTS READILY **EMBRACE** DRAWING," I ALSO WANT TO ACKNOWLEDGE THAT SOME STUDENTS WILL ALSO CLAIM **THEY DON'T KNOW HOW TO DRAW** OR THEY **AREN'T VERY GOOD** AT IT.

**HOWEVER**, THERE ARE **TWO REASONS** WHY I THINK THE VISUAL FORMATS I PRESENT IN THIS BOOK WORK: BECAUSE THEY ARE **SIMPLE** (THEY DON'T REQUIRE GREAT SKILL TO RECREATE) AND THEY ARE **ICONIC** (THEY ARE MEMORABLE). **HANDMADE THINKING**, AFTER ALL, IS CLOSER TO **DOODLING** THAN TO **DA VINCI**.

I'VE ALSO LEARNED THAT STUDENTS NEED HELP IN PICTURING **WHAT'S POSSIBLE**. AND THAT'S WHAT THIS BOOK IS ABOUT, TOO: **POSSIBILITIES.**

(FOR A MORE **DETAILED DISCUSSION** OF THE IDEAS PRESENTED IN THIS BOOK, SEE MY **NOTES** AT END OF THE BOOK.)

I'M INTERESTED IN **TWO PROBLEMS** I'VE ENCOUNTERED IN THE ENGLISH CLASSROOM.

AND WHEN I SAY **THE ENGLISH CLASSROOM**, I MEAN ANY CLASS: WRITING OR LITERATURE, UNDERGRADUATE OR GRADUATE.

BUT I KNOW THESE PROBLEMS EXIST IN **OTHER DISCIPLINES** AND AT **OTHER LEVELS** AS WELL.

MANY STUDENTS **DON'T READ** WHAT THEY ARE ASSIGNED TO READ.

AND MANY STUDENTS DON'T **ENGAGE** THE TEXTS THEY DO READ IN *A **CRITICAL*** WAY.

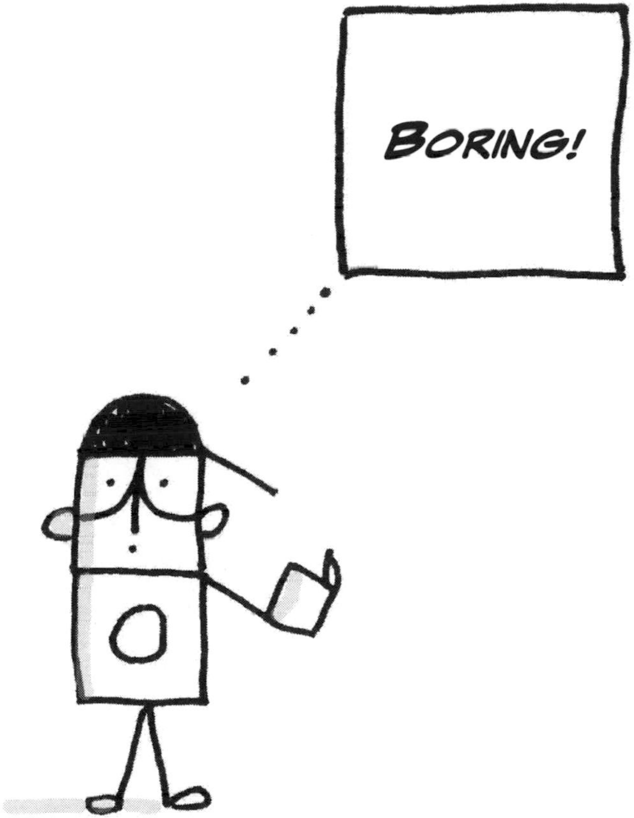
BORING!

HOW CAN WE CREATE MORE **ENGAGED** AND **CRITICAL** READERS?

SOME TEACHERS GIVE STUDENTS **POP-QUIZZES.**

SOME TEACHERS GIVE STUDENTS *PARTICIPATION POINTS.*

SOME TEACHERS HAVE STUDENTS **WRITE DAILY RESPONSES** ABOUT WHAT THEY HAVE READ.

I **DO** THIS.

WHEN I HAVE STUDENTS WRITE, I ASK THEM TO WRITE A **SUMMARY**, IDENTIFY A **SIGNIFICANT IDEA**, AND ASK A **QUESTION** ABOUT WHAT THEY'VE READ.

SOME TEACHERS HAVE STUDENTS **DRAW** THEIR RESPONSES.

I ALSO **DO** THIS.

I THINK STUDENTS CAN BENEFIT FROM **THINKING VISUALLY** ABOUT WHAT THEY'VE READ.

BY **VISUAL THINKING,** I MEAN THE ABILITY TO **THINK WITH** AND **ABOUT IMAGES.**

VISUAL THINKING INCLUDES A NUMBER OF COGNITIVE PROCESSES, INCLUDING THE **ANALYSIS, MANIPULATION,** AND **CREATION** OF IMAGES.

WHEN WE READ A MAP, WE ARE USING OUR VISUAL THINKING SKILLS TO **DISCOVER** WHERE WE ARE AND WHERE WE WANT TO GO. **SELECTING** APPROPRIATE COLORS FOR A BEDROOM OR **CUTTING AND PASTING** CLIP ART IMAGES INTO A PRESENTATION WOULD ALSO BE CONSIDERED VISUAL THINKING.

BUT I AM MORE INTERESTED IN HAVING STUDENTS **THINK WITH** IMAGES IN RESPONSE TO WHAT I ASK THEM TO READ.

THAT IS, I HAVE THEM USE **DRAWING** AS **A WAY OF THINKING** ABOUT WHAT THEY'VE READ.

I CALL THIS **HANDMADE THINKING.**

IT IS A **CREATIVE PROCESS:** THE DRAWING OF **NEW IMAGES** BY HAND IN ORDER TO **RESPOND** TO A SPECIFIC EXPERIENCE OR TO **SHOW** OUR THINKING TO OTHERS.

I USE **HANDMADE THINKING** IN THREE WAYS.

FIRST, I USE IT IN **MY RESEARCH.**

FOR SEVERAL YEARS, I'VE ASKED STUDENTS TO DRAW A PICTURE OF **WHAT HAPPENS WHEN THEY READ.**

MY STUDY OF THESE DRAWINGS HAS REVEALED **NINE METAPHORS** WE REGULARLY USE WHEN WE TALK AND THINK ABOUT READING:

**ENTERING, ABSORBING, MAKING,**

**TRAVELING, CHANGING, MOVING,**

**LIBERATING, BELIEVING, & STRENGTHENING**

I ALSO USE **HANDMADE THINKING** IN MY TEACHING.

I USE *IMAGES I'VE DRAWN* TO ILLUSTRATE CONCEPTS I WANT STUDENTS TO LEARN, SUCH AS **NINE WAYS** TO RESPOND TO LITERATURE:

PERSONAL, FORMAL, TOPICAL,

BIOGRAPHICAL, CONTEXTUAL, READER RESPONSE,

CREATIVE, INTERPRETIVE, & ETHICAL.

I ALSO ASSIGN **HANDMADE THINKING** TO MY STUDENTS.

I ASK THEM **TO DRAW** THEIR RESPONSES TO WHAT THEY READ TO PROMOTE **ENGAGED** AND **ANALYTICAL** READING HABITS.

THESE DRAWINGS ARE IN RESPONSE TO **MANY KINDS** OF TEXTS:

**NOVELS, SHORT STORIES, ESSAYS, POEMS, SCHOLARLY ARTICLES, & TEXTBOOK CHAPTERS.**

MY IDEAS ABOUT USING HANDMADE THINKING IN ENGLISH BEGAN AFTER I READ DAN ROAM'S GREAT BOOK **THE BACK OF THE NAPKIN.**

**DAN ROAM** ARGUES THAT DRAWING CAN BE **A POWERFUL TOOL** FOR PROBLEM-SOLVING AND PRESENTING ONE'S IDEAS TO OTHERS.

**ROAM** ARGUES THERE ARE SIX BASIC WAYS TO **SEE** THE WORLD AROUND US AND SIX WAYS TO **SHOW** WHAT WE'VE DISCOVERED.

THESE **SIX WAYS** GENERALLY CORRESPOND TO WHAT ARE TRADITIONALLY KNOWN AS THE **JOURNALIST'S QUESTIONS.**

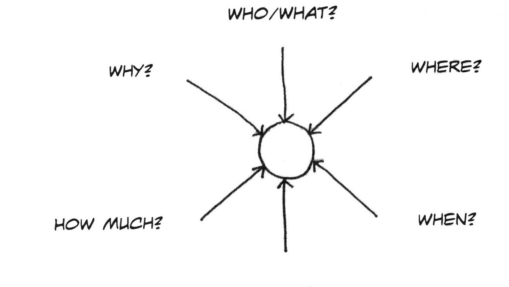

AND THESE SIX QUESTIONS CORRESPOND TO SIX WAYS OF *VISUALIZING INFORMATION.*

1. PORTRAIT
2. MAP
3. TIMELINE
4. PROCESS CHART
5. BAR GRAPH
6. MULTIVARIABLE GRAPH

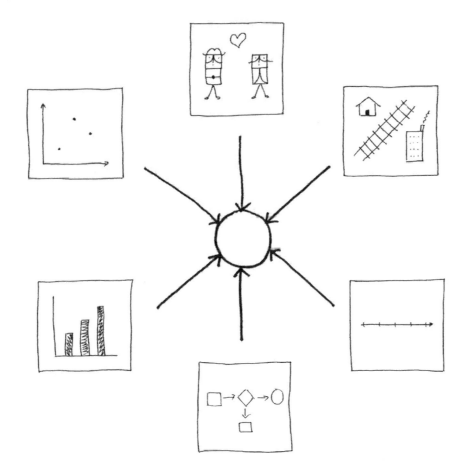

WHEN I DECIDED TO **EXPERIMENT** WITH DAN ROAM'S IDEAS IN MY OWN TEACHING (THAT IS, TO HAVE MY STUDENTS **ILLUSTRATE** THEIR RESPONSES TO READING ASSIGNMENTS), I DECIDED I WANTED TO USE **MORE THAN SIX** BASIC WAYS OF SEEING AND PRESENTING INFORMATION.

OVER TIME, I DEVELOPED **TWENTY-ONE** VISUAL FORMATS IN **FIVE** GROUPS.

AS YOU WILL SEE, THESE FORMATS ARE QUITE SIMPLE **BLACK AND WHITE** DRAWINGS. FOR WAYS MY STUDENTS HAVE USED THESE FORMATS, SEE MY SITE **WWW.HANDMADETHINKING.COM.**

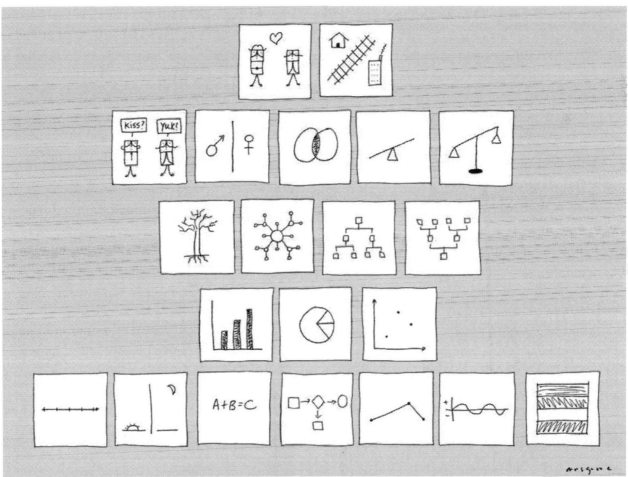

THE FIRST GROUP INCLUDED THOSE SIMILAR TO DAN ROAM'S **PORTRAITS** AND **MAPS**.

WE COULD ALSO THINK OF THESE AS THE **NOUN** GROUP.

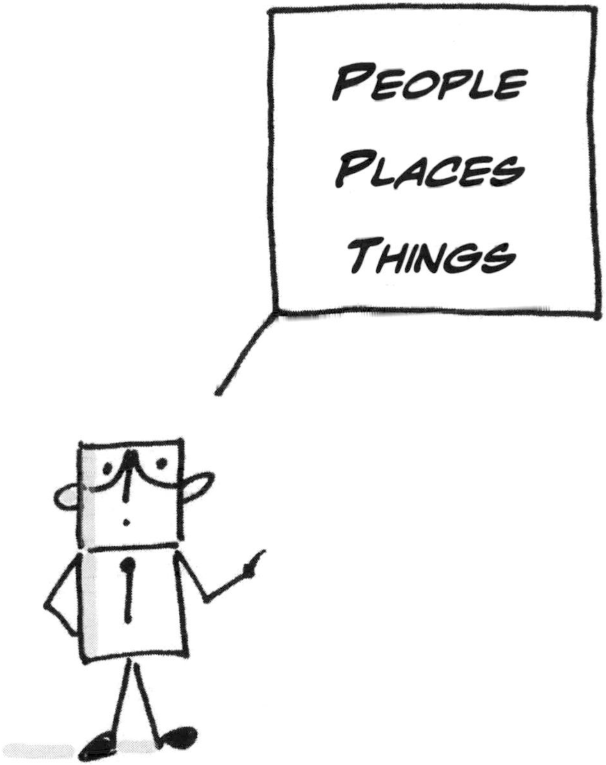
PEOPLE
PLACES
THINGS

PORTRAIT

MAP

THE NEXT GROUP INCLUDES IMAGES IN *PAIRS*.

THIS A **COMIC** PANEL
WITH TWO PEOPLE IN DIALOGUE.

# COMPARISON/CONTRAST

# VENN DIAGRAM

# SEESAW

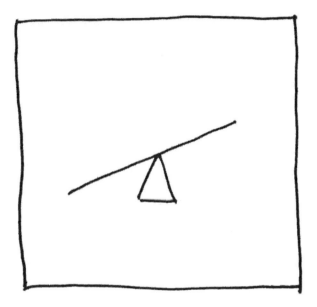

*SCALE*

SOME IMAGES INDICATE THE **GROWTH** OF AND **RELATIONSHIP** BETWEEN IDEAS.

*LIKE A TREE*

# THE COMMON *WEB* FOR BRAINSTORMING AND *MIND-MAPPING*

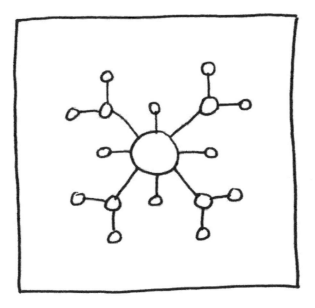

# THE ORGANIZATIONAL CHART

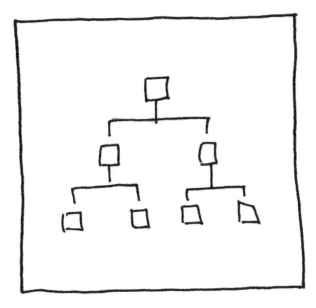

WHICH BECOMES **A GENEALOGICAL CHART**
IF YOU FLIP IT

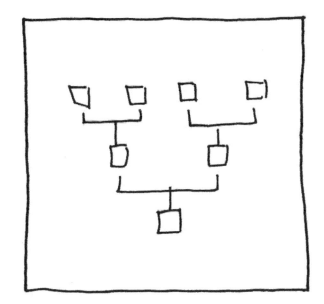

THERE ARE IMAGES THAT SHOW,
LIKE DAN ROAM SAYS,
**QUANTITIES** OR HOW MUCH.

# PIE CHART

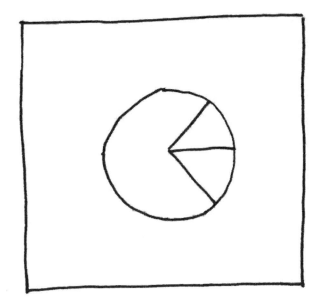

AND *MULTIVARIABLE GRAPH*

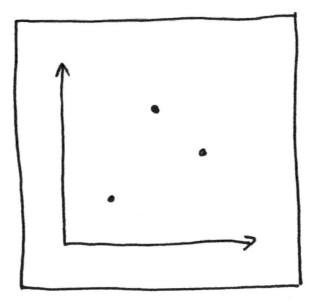

AND FINALLY, SOME IMAGES SHOW A **PROGRESSION** OVER TIME.

# TIMELINE

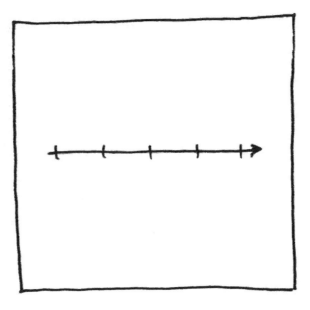

# BEFORE AND AFTER

## (COULD ALSO FIT IN THE **PAIRS** CATEGORY)

# THE EQUATION

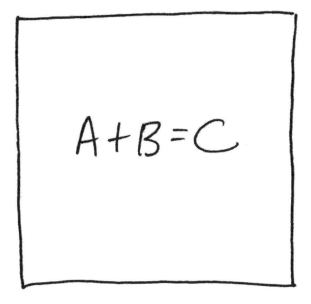

# A FLOW CHART

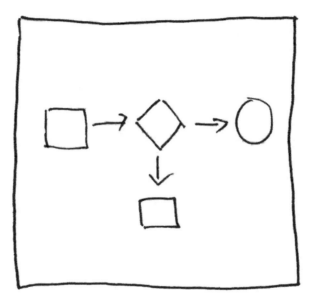

FREYTAG'S PYRAMID PLOT LINE

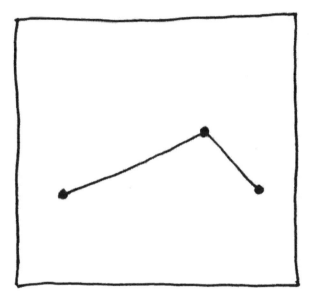

THIS IS **ANOTHER MULTIVARIABLE GRAPH** OR **+/- PLOT LINE** THAT SHOWS PROGRESSION UP AND DOWN AND LEFT TO RIGHT.

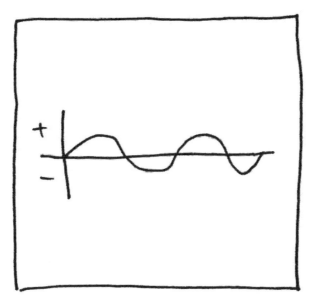

THIS IMAGE DEPICTS **LAYERS**, LIKE **SEDIMENT** MOVING FROM BOTTOM TO TOP.

HERE THEY ARE AGAIN:
**TWENTY-ONE** VISUAL FORMATS
FOR **HANDMADE THINKING**
IN **FIVE** GROUPS.

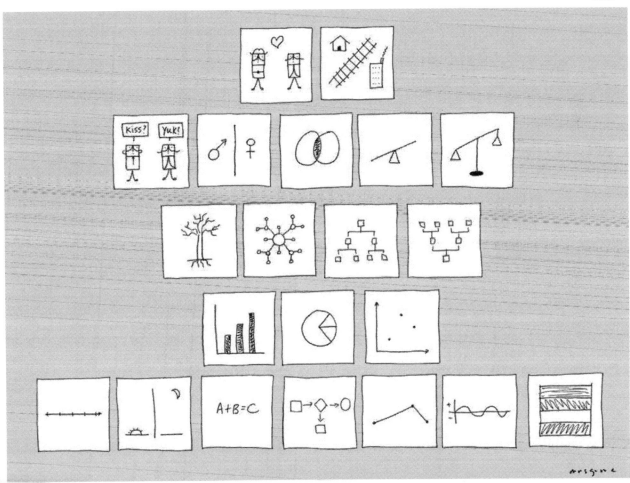

AGAIN, I ENCOURAGE YOU TO EXAMINE THE MANY **EXAMPLES** OF STUDENTS' HANDMADE RESPONSES ON **WWW.HANDMADETHINKING.COM.**

THESE DRAWINGS SHOW **THE VARIETY OF WAYS** MY STUDENTS HAVE USED THE TWENTY-ONE VISUAL FORMATS TO DEPICT THEIR RESPONSES TO READING ASSIGNMENTS, BOTH TO **LITERARY AND NON-LITERARY TEXTS.**

HERE ARE THE **GUIDELINES** FOR HANDMADE RESPONSES I USE IN MY CLASSES:

IN RESPONSE TO THE ASSIGNED READING, DRAW A PICTURE ON AN 8.5 X 11 SHEET OF PLAIN WHITE PAPER THAT CREATIVELY AND ORIGINALLY REPRESENTS THE AUTHOR'S ARGUMENT, NARRATIVE, OR COMPELLING IDEA.

THIS PICTURE SHOULD BE A COMBINATION OF IMAGES, WORDS, AND COLORS IN THE WHITE SPACE OF THE PAGE.

THE DRAWING MUST BE AN ORIGINAL DRAWING, FOLLOW ONE OR MORE OF THE TWENTY-ONE VISUAL FORMATS, AND INCLUDE NO CLIP ART.

WHICHEVER HANDMADE RESPONSE FORMAT YOU SELECT, YOUR DRAWING SHOULD BE PRESENTED IN LANDSCAPE FORMAT, BE EFFECTIVELY DEVELOPED, AND INCLUDE AT LEAST THREE COLORS (BLACK MAY BE ONE OF THOSE COLORS).

ON THE REVERSE OF THE READING VISUAL IN THE TOP LEFT CORNER, WRITE YOUR NAME, THE DATE, THE NAME OF THE READING ASSIGNMENT, AND THE NAME OF VISUAL FORMAT(S) YOU ARE USING.

ALSO ON THE REVERSE, INCLUDE AT LEAST ONE BRIEF CITATION FROM THE ASSIGNED TEXT (ALONG WITH THE PARENTHETICAL PAGE REFERENCE) THAT CORRESPONDS TO YOUR DRAWING.

AND HERE ARE THE **EVALUATION CRITERIA** I USE WHEN GRADING HANDMADE RESPONSES:

**5 POINTS:** EXCELLENT REPRESENTATION OF THE AUTHOR'S ARGUMENT, NARRATIVE, OR COMPELLING IDEA, INCLUDING CREATIVE AND EFFECTIVE BALANCE OF IMAGES, WORDS, AND COLOR; EXCELLENT AND EFFECTIVE IDEA DEVELOPMENT; AS WELL AS CORRECT CITATION AND PAGE REFERENCE; NO ERRORS IN SENTENCE, SPELLING, AND USAGE; ADHERENCE TO PAGE FORMAT FOR READING RESPONSE VISUALS.

**4 POINTS:** GOOD REPRESENTATION OF THE AUTHOR'S ARGUMENT, NARRATIVE, OR COMPELLING IDEA, INCLUDING CREATIVE AND EFFECTIVE BALANCE OF IMAGES, WORDS, AND COLOR; GOOD AND EFFECTIVE IDEA DEVELOPMENT; AS WELL AS CORRECT CITATION AND PAGE REFERENCE; NO ERRORS IN SENTENCE, SPELLING, AND USAGE; ADHERENCE TO PAGE FORMAT FOR READING RESPONSE VISUALS.

**3 POINTS:** SAME AS 4 BUT WITH INCORRECT FORMAT FOR CITATION, PAGE REFERENCE, OR PAGE FORMAT; OR MORE THAN TWO ERRORS IN SENTENCE, SPELLING, AND USAGE.

**1 POINT:** PERFUNCTORY VISUAL RESPONSE; FREQUENT ERRORS IN SENTENCE, SPELLING, AND USAGE; FAILURE TO INCLUDE ADEQUATE
IDEA DEVELOPMENT OR CITATION, OR TO ADHERE TO PAGE FORMAT OF READING RESPONSE VISUALS.

# CONCLUSION

**MY PURPOSE** HAS BEEN TO RECOMMEND **HANDMADE THINKING** AS AN **ADDITIONAL** WAY FOR STUDENTS TO **ENGAGE** AND **RESPOND** TO TEXTS.

I HAVE FOUND THAT AS STUDENTS **PRACTICE** THESE VISUAL FORMATS, MANY WILL **COMBINE** VISUAL FORMATS, SUCH AS THE TIMELINE AND PIE CHART, OR THE PORTRAIT AND THE MULTIVARIABLE GRAPH.

I'VE ALSO BEEN ESPECIALLY IMPRESSED WITH THE **CREATIVE** WAYS SOME STUDENTS HAVE USED THE **VENN DIAGRAM** TO DEPICT THEIR RESPONSES.

I HOPE YOU WILL **EXPERIMENT** WITH **HANDMADE THINKING** YOURSELF TO SEE HOW IT MIGHT SUPPORT **TEACHING AND LEARNING** IN YOUR DISCIPLINE.

I ALSO HOPE THAT YOU WILL **SHARE** WITH ME YOUR DRAWINGS AND **EXAMPLES** FROM YOUR STUDENTS.

IT'S ALSO **POSSIBLE** THAT YOU WILL DISCOVER **NEW VISUAL FORMATS** AS WELL. **SEND** ME THOSE, TOO!

114

# *NOTES*

**7.** I DISCOVERED THIS CITATION FROM D. R. AUGSBURG IN *THE CANADA EDUCATIONAL MONTHLY AND "SCHOOL MAGAZINE"* OF 1894.

**11.** YES, THIS IS A *PICTURE BOOK*. WHEN I BEGAN THINKING ABOUT THE BEST WAY TO PRESENT MY IDEAS ABOUT THE *POWER OF DRAWING AND IMAGES* IN THE CLASSROOM, I DECIDED I WANTED TO COMPOSE A *FAIRLY BASIC EXPLANATION* OF *HANDMADE THINKING* ILLUSTRATED WITH *MY OWN DRAWINGS*. I ALSO DECIDED THAT I WANTED MY READERS TO BE ABLE TO READ MY BOOK RATHER *QUICKLY* AND NOT BE WEIGHED DOWN WITH THE TRADITIONAL ACADEMIC REVIEW OF RELATED MATERIALS. IN THE LONG RUN, I WANTED A *SIMPLE* AND *DIRECT* EXPLANATION OF HOW THE *MARRIAGE OF DRAWING AND READING* CAN CREATE MORE *ENGAGED AND CRITICAL READERS.*

**11.** BY HELPING STUDENTS LEARN *WHAT'S POSSIBLE* (RATHER THAN THE RIGHT ANSWER FOR EVERY TEXT), TEACHERS *EMPOWER* STUDENTS AS CRITICAL THINKERS AND READERS. AND BY PROVIDING STUDENTS WITH *CHOICES* FOR DRAWING, I HOPE THEY WILL ALSO BECOME *BETTER DECISION-MAKERS* AND BUILD MORE *FRUITFUL RELATIONSHIPS* WITH READING.

**11.** I WOULD ALSO POINT TO *THREE EXCELLENT RESOURCES* TO EASE STUDENTS' MINDS ABOUT DRAWING:

    A. *ED EMBERLEY'S* BOOK *MAKE A WORLD*. EMBERLEY'S SIMPLE *STEP-BY-STEP INSTRUCTIONS* FOR COMBINING LINES AND SHAPES INTO AN ENDLESS NUMBER OF *FIGURES* DEMONSTRATES JUST HOW *EASY* DRAWING CAN BE. *EMBERLEY'S BOOK* SHOULD BE ON EVERYONE'S *REFERENCE SHELF.*

B. **OTHER STUDENTS' DRAWINGS.** WHENEVER POSSIBLE, I SHARE **EXCEPTIONAL EXAMPLES** OF STUDENT DRAWINGS WITH THE CLASS, EITHER INCORPORATED IN THE DAY'S AGENDA VIA POWERPOINT OR ON A DOCUMENT CAMERA. CONTINUALLY DEMONSTRATING **WHAT'S POSSIBLE** ALWAYS HELPS.

C. **YOUR DRAWINGS.** ANY **LIVE PERFORMANCE** OF DRAWING SIMPLE FIGURES FOR YOUR STUDENTS WILL SHOW THEM JUST HOW EASY IT IS. LOOK AGAIN AT PAGE 15 AND THE FIGURE OF **PROFESSOR QUADRANGLE** I'VE MADE FOR THIS BOOK. HE'S **TWO SQUARES** WITH LEGS, PLUS SOME DETAILS. AGAIN, SEE EMBERLEY'S **MAKE A WORLD.**

14. I BELIEVE THESE PROBLEMS EXIST IN **ANY COURSE** THAT REQUIRES READING. THUS, THE **HANDMADE THINKING STRATEGIES** OUTLINED IN THIS BOOK SHOULD FACILITATE STUDENT LEARNING IN THOSE COURSES, TOO.

30. IN MY CLASSES, I HAVE STUDENTS **ALTERNATE** BETWEEN WRITTEN AND HANDMADE RESPONSES.

34. WHILE THIS BOOK FOCUSES ON **HANDMADE THINKING** AS A **READING RESPONSE** ACTIVITY, YOU COULD ALSO HAVE STUDENTS USE HANDMADE THINKING WHEN **REFLECTING** ON A TOPIC AND AS A **PREWRITING** TOOL. BY THAT I MEAN, STUDENTS CAN **DRAW IN CLASS TO GATHER THEIR THOUGHTS** AND **TO SKETCH OUT** THE FOCUS, ORGANIZATION, AND DEVELOPMENT OF THEIR WRITING PROJECTS PRIOR TO COMPOSING A FIRST DRAFT.

38. FOR MORE ON MY RESEARCH INTO THE METAPHORS WE READ BY, SEE MY FORTHCOMING PICTURE BOOK **METAPHORS WE READ BY.**

40. FOR MORE ON THE WAYS I TEACH LITERARY RESPONSE, SEE MY FORTHCOMING PICTURE BOOK **PICTURING A READER'S RESPONSIBILITIES.**

**44.** IN FACT, BEFORE I ENCOUNTERED *THE BACK OF THE NAPKIN,* I OFTEN ASKED MY STUDENTS TO USE DRAWING TO *CAPTURE AND COMMUNICATE* THEIR IDEAS, BUT THE NOTION OF *WEAVING* HANDMADE THINKING ASSIGNMENTS *THROUGHOUT A COURSE* DIDN'T REALLY HIT ME UNTIL I READ ROAM'S BOOK.

**50.** WHILE ROAM ARGUES THAT THERE ARE *SIX BASIC WAYS* OF SEEING AND PRESENTING INFORMATION, HE ALSO USES *MORE THAN SIX BASIC WAYS* TO REPRESENT WHAT WE SEE AND PRESENT. STILL, THE *TWENTY-ONE VISUAL FORMATS* AS I'VE ORGANIZED AND PRESENTED IN THIS BOOK GO WELL BEYOND THE VISUAL FORMATS HE USES.

**54.** MANY STUDENTS ARE ATTRACTED TO THE *PORTRAIT* FORMAT. HOWEVER, PORTRAITS TEND TOWARD *SIMPLE ILLUSTRATIONS* OF CHARACTERS *RATHER THAN COMPLEX THINKING* ABOUT THEME OR RELATIONSHIPS BETWEEN CHARACTERS OR IDEAS. YOU MAY HAVE TELL STUDENTS WHO *GET STUCK* ON PORTRAITS *TO MOVE ON* TO ANOTHER VISUAL FORMAT.

**56.** I THINK *MAPS* ARE ALSO VERY ATTRACTIVE TO STUDENTS AS THEY *BEGIN EXPERIMENTING* WITH VISUAL FORMATS, ESPECIALLY IN RESPONSE TO *NARRATIVES.*

**60.** THE *COMIC PANEL* OR *CARTOON* IS A VERY PRODUCTIVE VISUAL FORMAT FOR STUDENTS, BUT STUDENTS CAN ALSO CREATE *MULTI-PANEL COMICS.* COMBINING THE *COMIC PANEL* WITH THE *BEFORE AND AFTER* VISUAL FORMAT OR THE *TIMELINE* ARE GOOD WAYS TO THINK ABOUT MULTI-PANEL COMICS. SEE ALSO *SCOTT MCCLOUD'S* EXCELLENT BOOK *UNDERSTANDING COMICS.*

**64.** MANY OF MY STUDENTS HAVE USED THE *VENN DIAGRAM* IN VERY PRODUCTIVE WAYS, ESPECIALLY WHEN THEY HAVE COMBINED THE *PORTRAIT* WITH THE *VENN DIAGRAM* FORMAT. IN SOME CASES, THEY HAVE *COMBINED* THE *PORTRAIT, COMPARISON/CONTRAST, AND VENN DIAGRAM* FORMATS IN ONE DRAWING.

**66.** THE *SEESAW* WAS A VISUAL FORMAT THAT I DID NOT INTRODUCE TO MY STUDENTS; YET, IT KEPT POPPING UP IN MANY OF THEIR DRAWINGS ANYWAY. THE *REPEATED APPEARANCE* OF THIS FORMAT WAS EVIDENCE THAT SOME STUDENTS NEEDED A WAY TO SHOW HOW *SOME IDEAS ARE IN BALANCE.* IT WAS ALSO EVIDENCE OF THE POWER OF HANDMADE THINKING TO HELP STUDENTS *COMMUNICATE RELATIONSHIPS THAT COULDN'T BE SHOWN OTHERWISE.*

**68.** THE *SCALE* FORMAT MAY BE QUITE SIMILAR TO THE *SEESAW* FORMAT, BUT MY STUDENTS GENERALLY HAVE USED THE SCALES TO REPRESENT *VALUES IN TENSION* RATHER THAN *IDEAS IN BALANCE.* IN EITHER CASE, I THINK THESE TWO FORMATS PROVIDE STUDENTS A WAY OF UNDERSTANDING AND REPRESENTING CONCEPTS AND CHARACTERS *NOT AS INDEPENDENT ABSOLUTES* (LIKE THE *COMPARISON/CONTRAST* FORMAT) BUT AS *MUTUALLY DEPENDENT RELATIONSHIPS.*

**72.** FOR SOME STUDENTS, THE *TREE* IS MORE PRODUCTIVE THAN THE *WEB* FORMAT FOR SHOWING THE DEVELOPMENT OF IDEAS. PERHAPS IT HAS TO DO WITH *VERTICAL GROWTH* RATHER THAN THE *CENTRIFUGAL* NATURE OF THE WEB.

**84.** SOME OF MY STUDENTS HAVE COMBINED THE *PIE CHART* WITH THE *TIMELINE* FORMAT IN INTERESTING WAYS, ESPECIALLY WHEN READING ABOUT *QUANTITATIVE CHANGES* OVER TIME.

**86.** THE *MULTIVARIABLE* GRAPH IS A FAIRLY COMPLEX FORMAT THAT MOST STUDENTS WON'T IMMEDIATELY CHOOSE. HOWEVER, AFTER DEMONSTRATING SOME RELATIVELY *SIMPLE EXAMPLES*, THEY SHOULD EMBRACE IT QUITE EASILY. SEE HTTP://WWW.THISISINDEXED.COM FOR SOME GREAT EXAMPLES.

**90.** THE *TIMELINE* FORMAT LOOKS PRETTY SIMPLE, BUT STUDENTS HAVE FOUND FASCINATING WAYS TO COMBINE THIS FORMAT WITH OTHERS, ESPECIALLY THE *PORTRAIT* AND *PIE CHART* FORMATS.

**94.** AFTER DEMONSTRATING EXAMPLES OF THE *EQUATION* FORMAT, SOME STUDENTS WILL FIND ENGAGING WAYS TO DEPICT THEIR RESPONSES. SOME INTERESTING EXAMPLES CAN BE FOUND AT HTTP://WWW.MORENEWMATH.COM. YOU MAY ALSO FIND THAT SOME STUDENTS CAN GET *STUCK* ON THIS FORMAT AND WILL NEED SOME *NUDGING* INTO OTHER FORMATS.

**96.** THE **FLOW CHART** FORMAT MAY REQUIRE A BIT OF EXPLANATION, ESPECIALLY THE **DECISION DIAMOND** THAT DEPENDS UPON A **POSITIVE/NEGATIVE** OR **TRUE/FALSE** CONDITION BEING MET.

**100.** THE **+/- PLOT LINE** IS MY PERSONAL FAVORITE RESPONSE FORMAT FOR **EXTENDED NARRATIVES.** I LEARNED ABOUT THIS FROM MY FRIEND **AUSTIN KLEON** WHO LEARNED IT FROM KURT VONNEGUT'S **PALM SUNDAY.** [I DON'T KNOW WHERE **KURT VONNEGUT** LEARNED IT.]

**102.** THE **LAYERS** FORMAT MAY ALSO BE A CANDIDATE FOR THE GROUP OF FORMATS I'VE TERMED **FAMILY.**

**104.** WHILE I'VE TRIED TO **ORGANIZE** THESE **TWENTY-ONE** FORMATS IN **FIVE GROUPS**, YOU MAY FIND THAT YOU WOULD GROUP AND NAME THEM **DIFFERENTLY.** HELP YOURSELF. AND IF YOU AND YOUR STUDENTS DISCOVER **NEW FORMATS** THAT ARE HELPFUL IN HANDMADE THINKING, **GO FOR IT. MY GOAL** HAS NOT BEEN TO **CONFINE** THE WAYS **WE THINK OR DRAW.** MY GOAL IS ALWAYS TO FIND **MORE PRODUCTIVE WAYS TO TEACH AND LEARN.**

# RESOURCES

## SOURCES I REFER TO IN THIS BOOK

D. R. AUGSBERG, *"DRAWING IN GENERAL EDUCATION"*

LYNDA BARRY, *WHAT IT IS*

CRAIG DAMRAUER, *HTTP://WWW.MORENEWMATH.COM*

ED EMBERLEY, *MAKE A WORLD*

MILTON GLASER, *DRAWING IS THINKING*

JESSICA HAGY, *HTTP://WWW.THISISINDEXED.COM*

AUSTIN KLEON, *HTTP://WWW.AUSTINKLEON.COM*

SCOTT MCCLOUD, *UNDERSTANDING COMICS*

DAN ROAM, *THE BACK OF THE NAPKIN*

KURT VONNEGUT, *PALM SUNDAY*

JEFFREY WILHELM, *READING IS SEEING*

## A VERY BRIEF LIST OF OTHER SOURCES ON VISUAL AND HANDMADE THINKING

FRAN CLAGGETT AND JOAN BROWN, *DRAWING YOUR OWN CONCLUSIONS: GRAPHIC STRATEGIES FOR READING, WRITING, AND THINKING*

COGNITIVE MEDIA, *HTTP://WWW.COGNITIVEMEDIA.CO.UK*

COMMON CRAFT, *HTTP://WWW.COMMONCRAFT.COM*

NANCY DUARTE, *HTTP://BLOG.DUARTE.COM*

BETTY EDWARDS, *THE NEW DRAWING ON THE RIGHT SIDE OF THE BRAIN*

WILL EISNER, *GRAPHIC STORYTELLING AND VISUAL NARRATIVE*

DAVE GRAY, *HTTP://WWW.DAVEGRAYINFO.COM*

NANCY MARGULIES, *MAPPING INNER SPACE*

EDWARD R. TUFTE, *THE COGNITIVE STYLE OF POWERPOINT: PITCHING OUT CORRUPTS WITHIN*

VIZTHINK, *WWW.VIZTHINK.COM*

# ABOUT THE AUTHOR

**LAURENCE MUSGROVE** IS PROFESSOR AND HEAD OF THE DEPARTMENT OF ENGLISH AT ANGELO STATE UNIVERSITY IN SAN ANGELO, TEXAS, WHERE HE TEACHES COURSES IN COMPOSITION, LITERATURE, CREATIVE WRITING, AND ENGLISH EDUCATION.

HIS WORK HAS BEEN PUBLISHED IN *INSIDE HIGHER ED, THE CHRONICLE OF HIGHER EDUCATION, JAEPL, SOUTHERN INDIANA REVIEW, CHRISTIANITY AND LITERATURE,* AND *CONCHO RIVER REVIEW.*

HE OFFERS *ONSITE WORKSHOPS* AND *WEBINARS* ON HANDMADE THINKING, READING RESPONSIBLY, AND METAPHORS WE READ BY.

HE ALSO *BLOGS* @ WWW.THEILLUSTRATEDPROFESSOR.COM AND WWW.CARTOONRANCH.COM.

HE IS COMPOSING TWO OTHER PICTURE BOOKS: *PICTURING A READER'S RESPONSIBILITIES* AND *METAPHORS WE READ BY.*